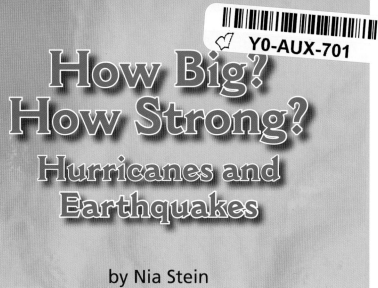

How Big?
How Strong?
Hurricanes and Earthquakes

by Nia Stein

PEARSON

Glenview, Illinois • Boston, Massachusetts • Chandler, Arizona
Upper Saddle River, New Jersey

hurricane

ocean

    Hurricanes and earthquakes are both natural disasters. They cause damage and hurt people. In some ways, hurricanes and earthquakes are similar. Of course, in some ways they are different.

    Hurricanes are huge ocean storms. Earthquakes are caused by a sudden movement in the earth.

---

natural disaster: terrible damage caused by nature

Hurricanes

Scientists who study the earth measure hurricanes. They find out the average wind speed of a hurricane to measure it. Then they use a system called the Saffir-Simpson Scale to show how strong the storm is. The higher the  number, the stronger the hurricane is. A Category 5 hurricane is the strongest and most destructive kind of hurricane.

---

wind speed: how fast the wind blows
destructive: damaging
scale: a way to measure something
measure: to learn how much of something there is

The Saffir-Simpson Scale

Type of Hurricane	Wind Speed in miles per hour (mph)
Category 1	74 to 95 mph
Category 2	96 to 110 mph
Category 3	111 to 130 mph
Category 4	131 to 155 mph
Category 5	more than 155 mph

Hurricane Andrew destroyed many buildings.

Hurricane Andrew was a Category 4 storm. Hurricane Andrew roared across the Atlantic Ocean in 1992. It was one of the worst storms ever to hit the United States. Its fastest winds were about 165 miles per hour. The strong winds and high tides destroyed buildings and property. Hurricane Andrew caused billions of dollars in damage.

roared: moved with great noise

Four hurricanes hit Florida in 2004.

Florida Hurricanes in 2004

Name	Strength	Date
Charley	Category 4	Aug. 13
Frances	Category 2	Sept. 5
Ivan	Category 3	Sept. 16
Jeanne	Category 3	Sept. 25

Once again, the hurricanes damaged buildings and property. The state was a disaster area.

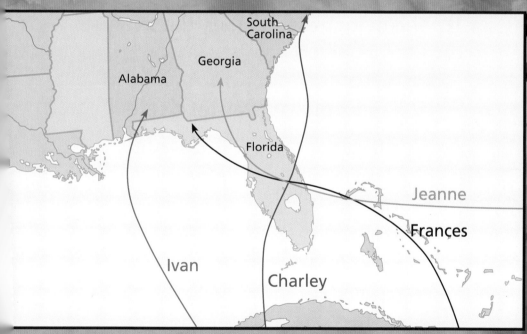

Paths of hurricanes Charley, Frances, Ivan, and Jeanne

disaster area: a place where terrible damage has happened

Earthquakes

When an earthquake happens, the ground shakes or slides. Some earthquakes are stronger than others and shake the ground harder than others. Scientists use a system called the Richter (RIK tur) Scale to measure the strength of an earthquake. The numbers on the Richter scale go up to 10. The higher the number, the stronger the earthquake is.

Sample of Richter Scale

Number	Damage
Lower than 4.3	Often no damage
4.4 to 4.8	Little damage
4.9 to 5.4	Some damage
6.0 to 6.5	Big damage
6.6 or higher	Major damage

Damage from the earthquake in California in 1994

Many earthquakes happen in the state of California. One earthquake happened there on January 17, 1994, near the city of San Francisco. This earthquake measured 6.7 on the Richter Scale. It caused 57 deaths. It caused more than 40 billion dollars in damage to property.

Damage from the earthquake in Alaska in 1964

The strongest earthquake in the U.S. happened in Alaska in 1964. It measured 8.6 on the Richter Scale. The strongest earthquake in the world happened in Chile in 1960. It measured 9.5 on the Richter Scale.

More than a million earthquakes happen each year. The good news is that most earthquakes are so small that no one even feels them!